I0606216

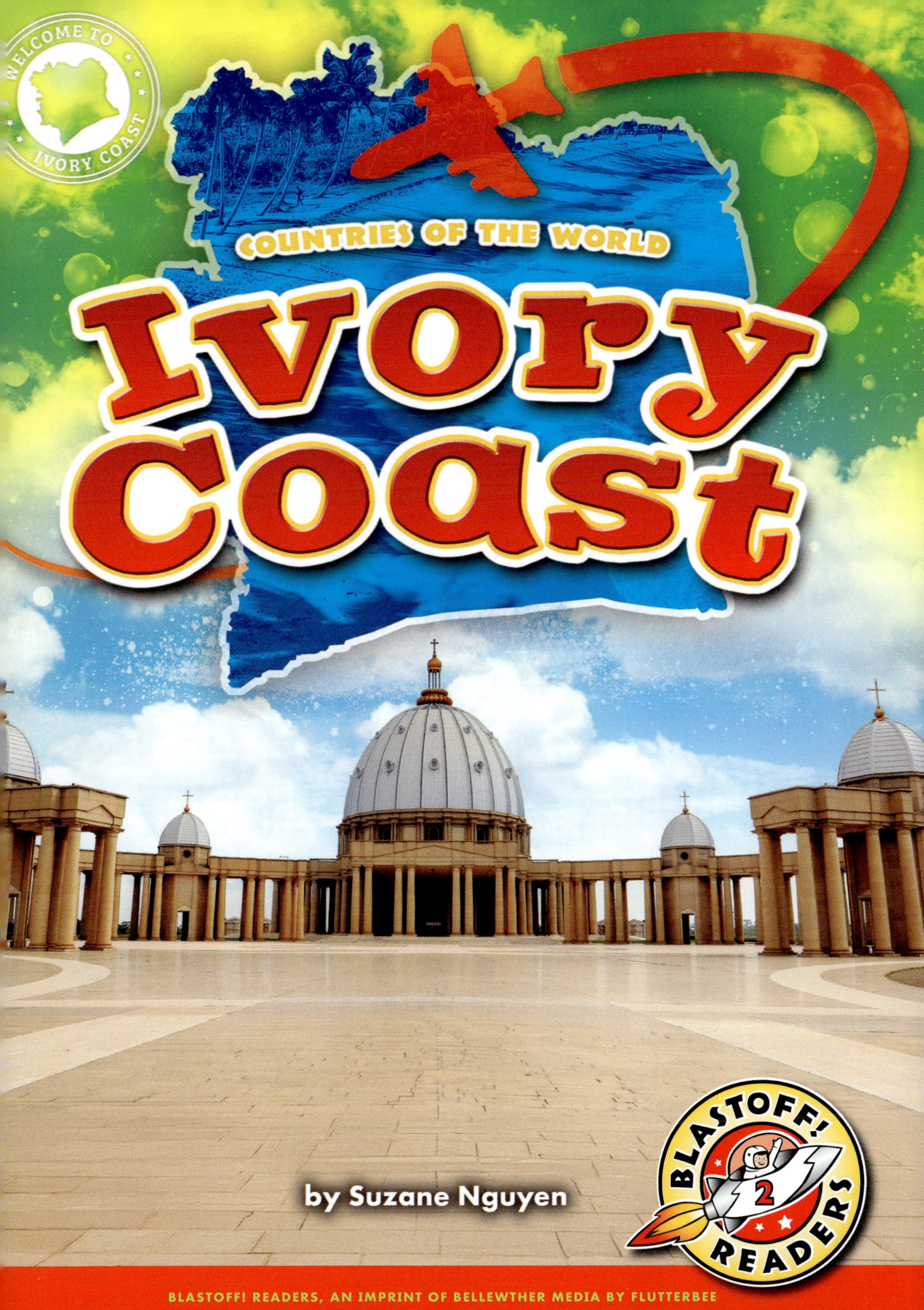

Ivory Coast

by Suzane Nguyen

BLASTOFF! READERS, AN IMPRINT OF BELLEWTHER MEDIA BY FLUTTERBEE

Blastoff! Readers are carefully developed by literacy experts to build reading stamina and move students toward fluency by combining standards-based content with developmentally appropriate text.

LEVELS

Level 1 provides the most support through repetition of high-frequency words, light text, predictable sentence patterns, and strong visual support.

Level 2 offers early readers a bit more challenge through varied sentences, increased text load, and text-supportive special features.

Level 3 advances early-fluent readers toward fluency through increased text load, less reliance on photos, advancing concepts, longer sentences, and more complex special features.

★ **Blastoff! Universe**

Reading Level

Grade K

Grades 1–3

Grade 4

This edition first published in 2026 by Bellwether Media, Inc.

Text copyright © 2026 by Bellwether Media, Inc. All rights reserved. No part of this publication may be reproduced, stored in any retrieval system, or transmitted in any form or by any means, electronic, mechanical, photocopying, recording, or otherwise, without written permission of the publisher.

BLASTOFF! READERS and associated logos are trademarks and/or registered trademarks of Bellwether Media, Inc. Bellwether Media is a division of FlutterBee Education Group.

For information regarding permission, write to Bellwether Media, Inc., Attention: Permissions Department, 3500 American Blvd W, Suite 150, Bloomington, MN 55431.

Library of Congress Cataloging-in-Publication Data is available at www.loc.gov or upon request from the publisher.

ISBN: 9798893047844 (hardcover)
ISBN: 9798893048841 (ebook)

Editor: Ashley Kuehl   Designer: Brittany McIntosh

Printed in the United States of America, North Mankato, MN.

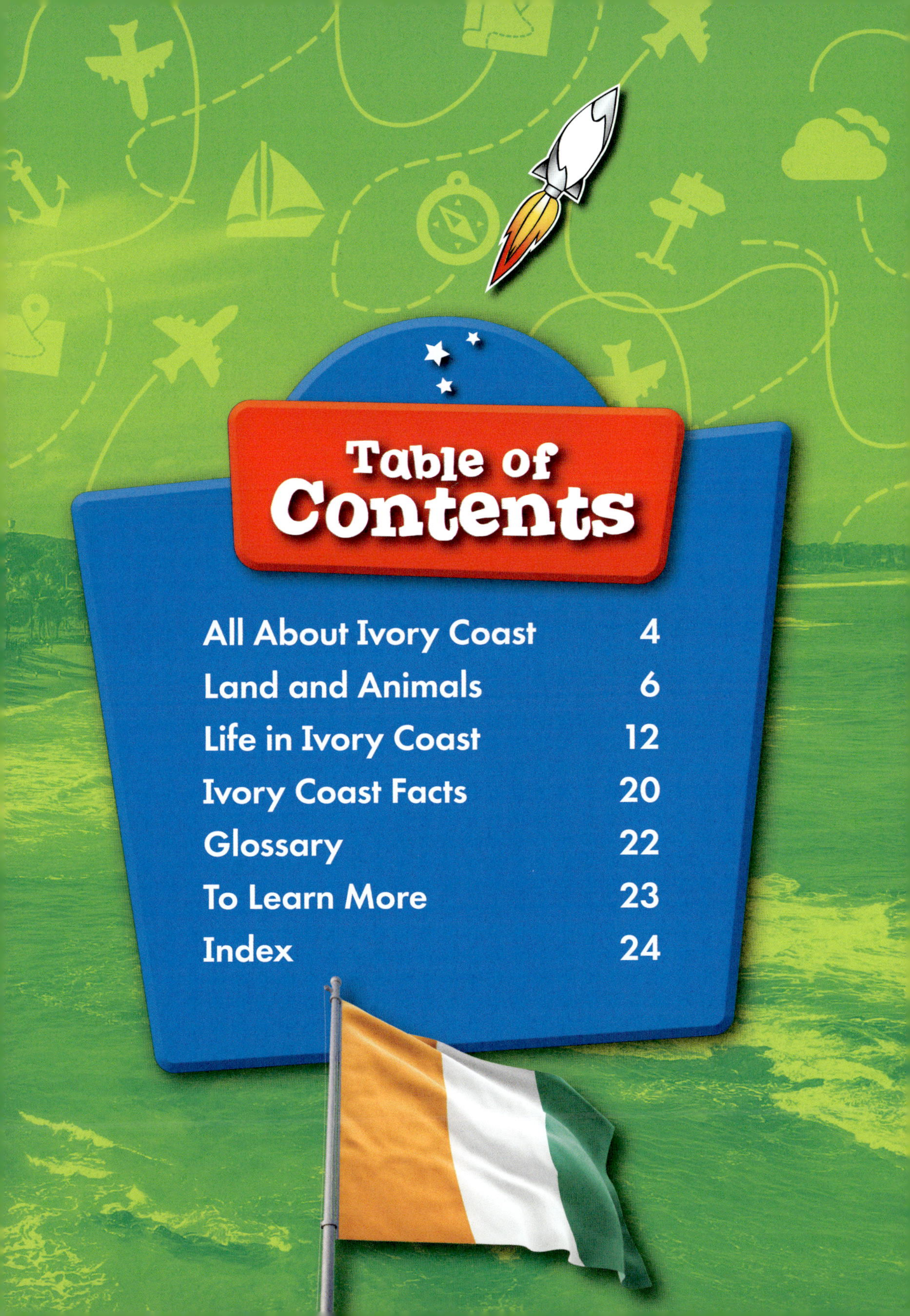

Table of Contents

All About Ivory Coast

Ivory Coast is a large country in West Africa. The capital is Yamoussoukro.

Côte d'Ivoire is the country's real name. In English, we say Ivory Coast.

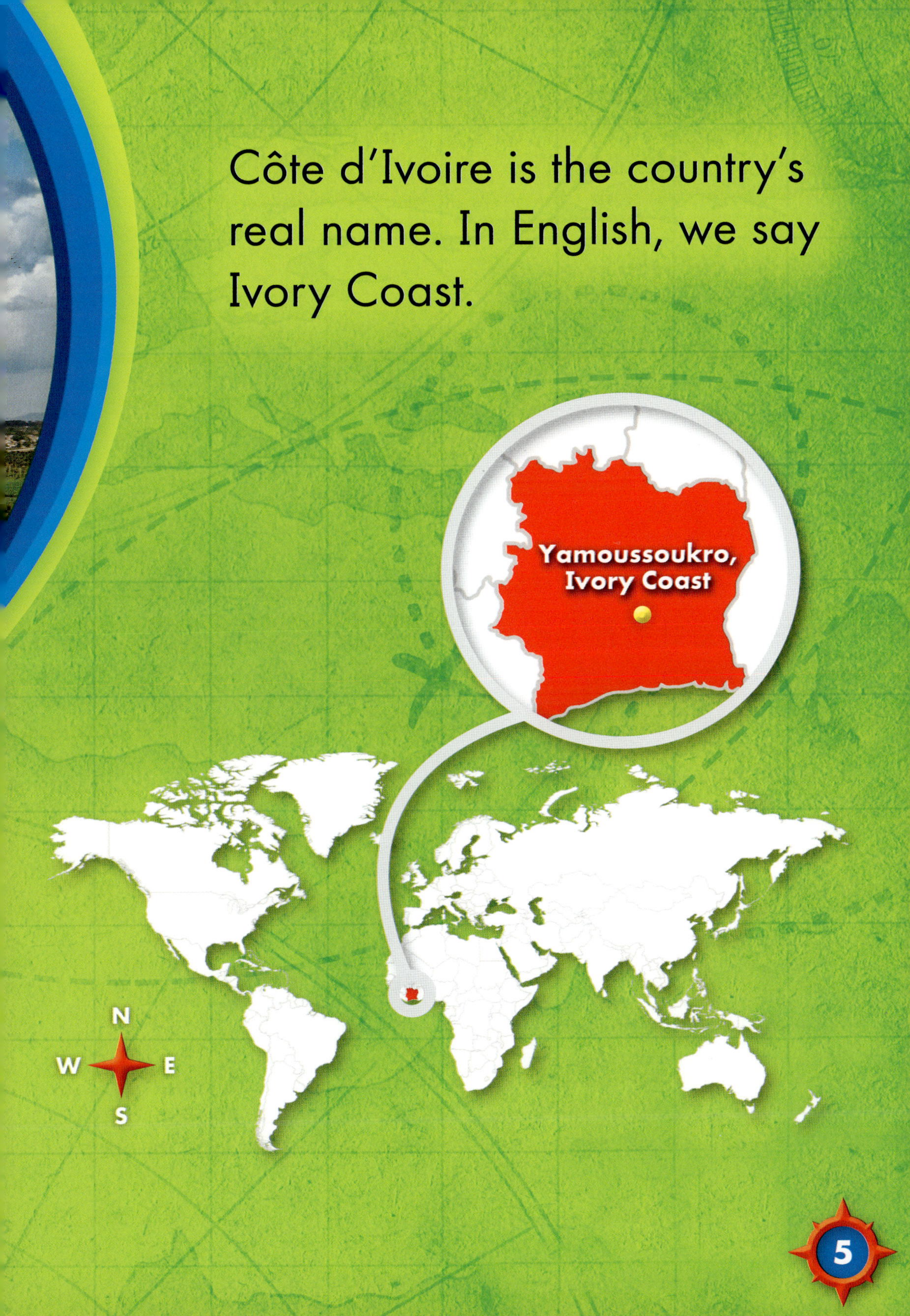

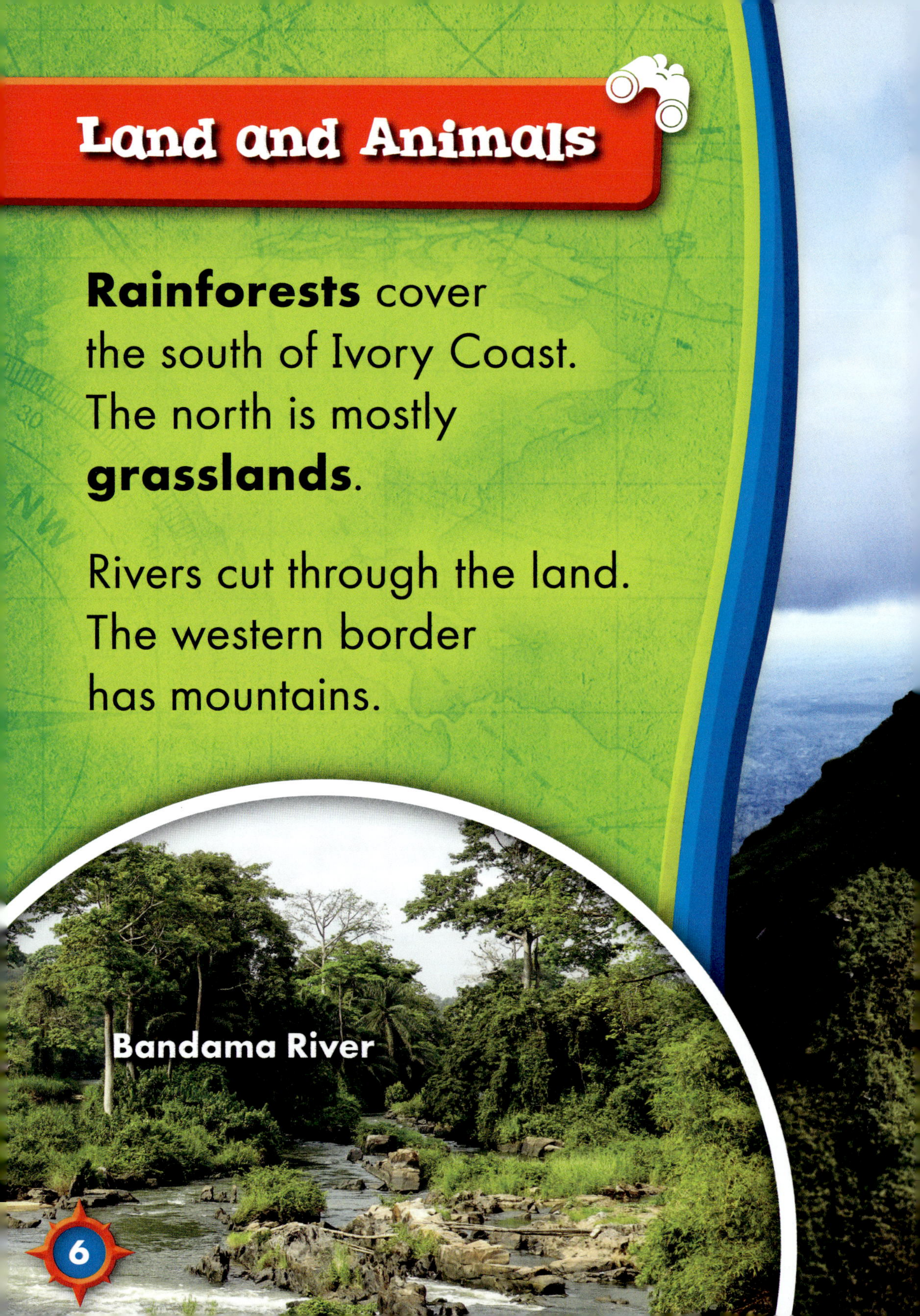

Land and Animals

Rainforests cover the south of Ivory Coast. The north is mostly **grasslands**.

Rivers cut through the land. The western border has mountains.

Bandama River

Mount Nimba

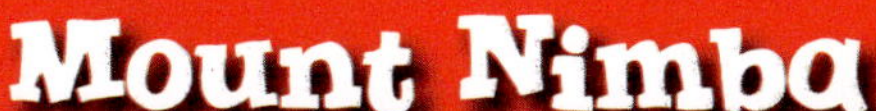

Size: 5,748 feet (1,752 meters) tall

Famous For: tallest mountain in Ivory Coast and borders two other countries

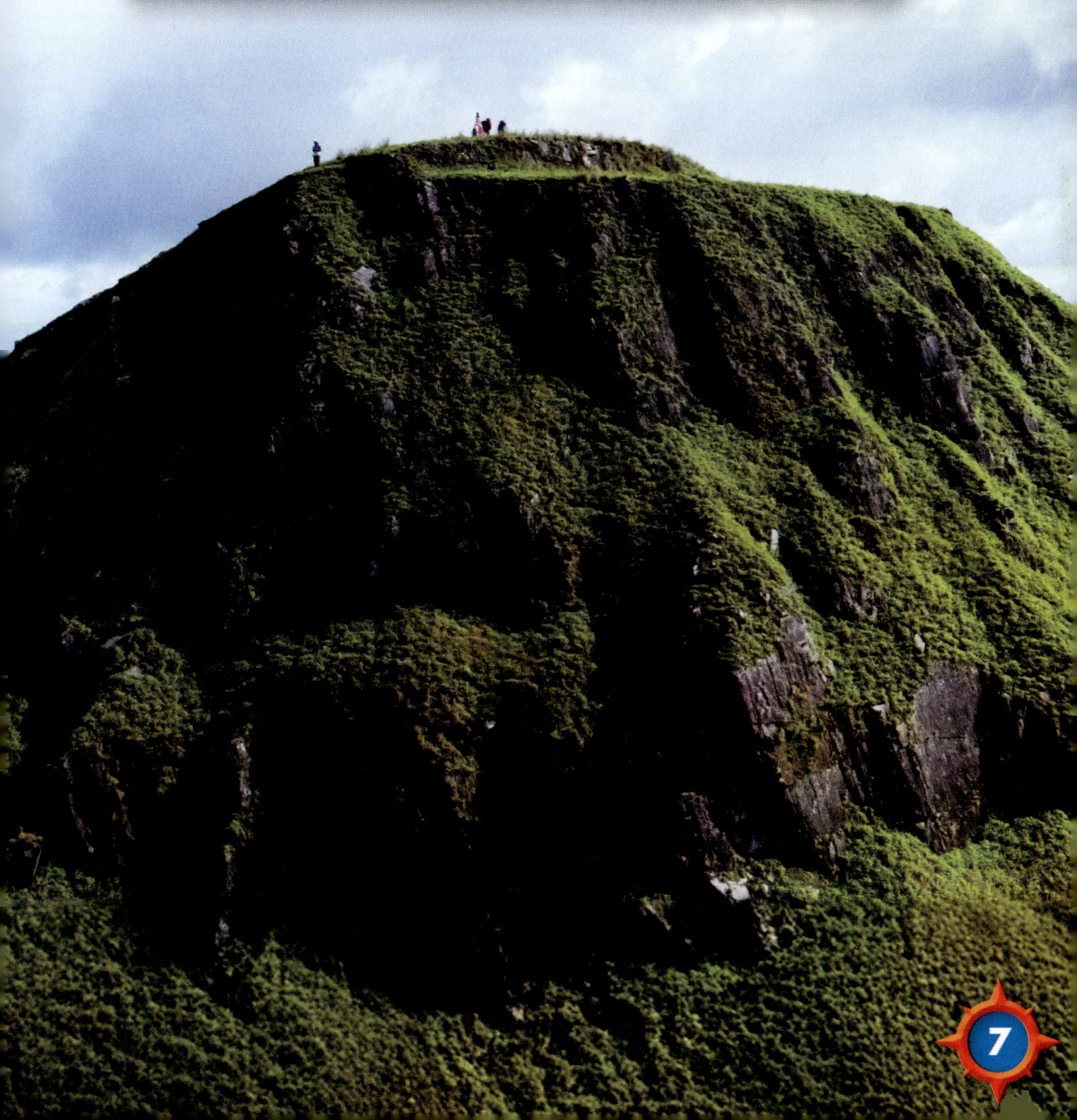

Ivory Coast is hot and **humid**. Different parts have different weather.

A lot of rain falls along the coast. The mountains are drier.

Ivory Coast is home to many animals. Chimpanzees swing through trees. Hippos rest in water.

African fish eagle

chimpanzee

pygmy hippo

African fish eagle

common agama

Eagles find fish in rivers.
Agamas hunt for bugs nearby.

Life in Ivory Coast

There are over 60 **ethnic** groups in Ivory Coast. Around half of Ivorians live in cities.

Most Ivorians speak French. They also speak more than 70 **Indigenous** languages.

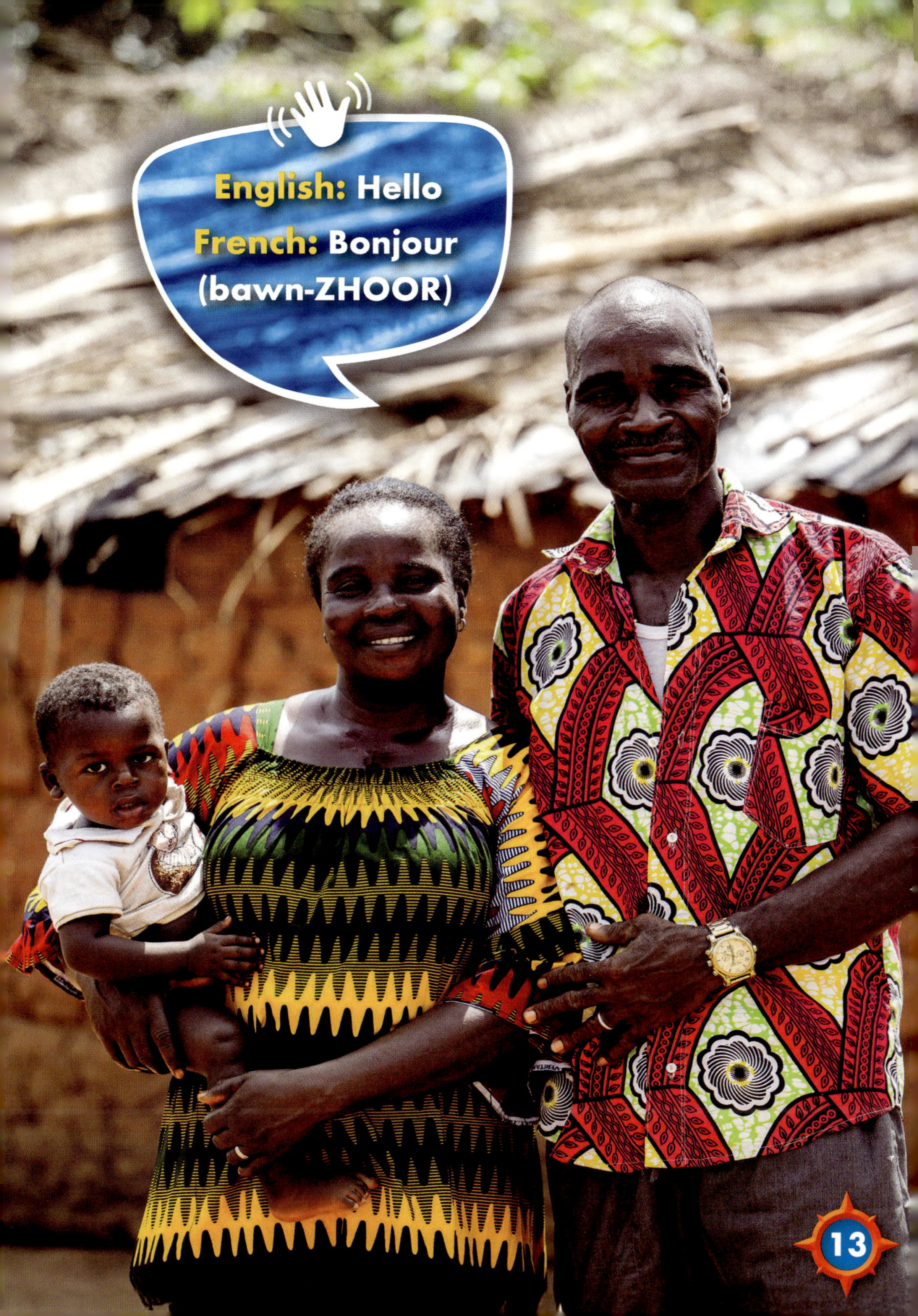
English: Hello
French: Bonjour
(bawn-ZHOOR)

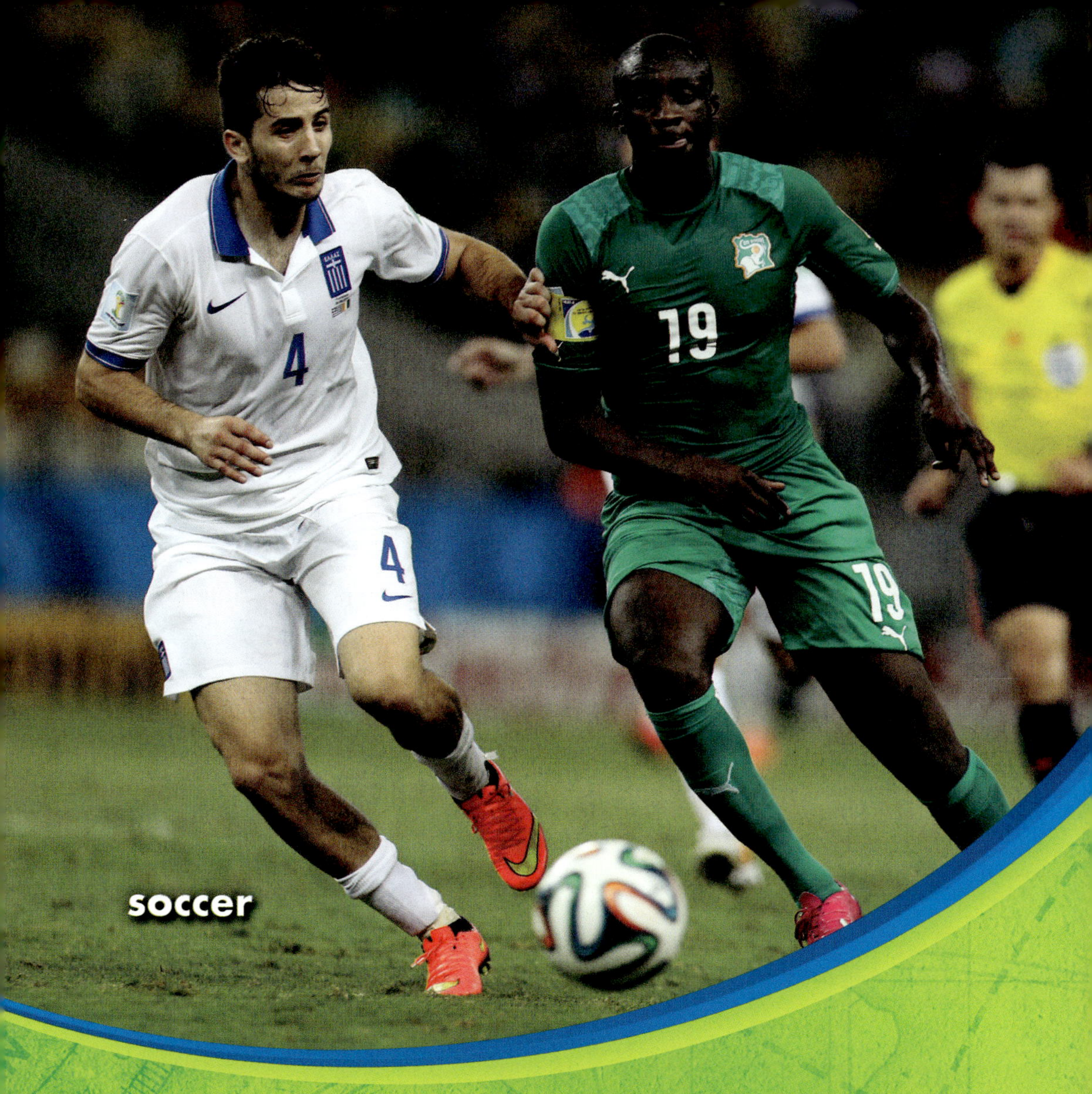

soccer

Soccer is the most popular sport in Ivory Coast. People play basketball and other sports too.

Young adults enjoy watching movies. *Awale* is a popular board game.

awale

Sauce *d'arachide* is a peanut sauce on rice. *Attiéké* is made from **cassava**.

Alloco is fried **plantain**.
Bofloto is a donut.

Independence Day is on August 7. There are parades and music.

Festival of Masks happens every year. People wear colorful masks and dance. Ivorians are proud of their country!

Ivory Coast Facts

Size:
124,504 square miles
(322,463 square kilometers)

Population:
33,180,000 (2025)

National Holiday:
Independence Day (August 7)

Main Language:
French

Capital City:
Yamoussoukro

Famous Face

Name: Didier Drogba

Famous For: one of the most successful soccer players of all time

Religions

none: 19%

Muslim: 43%

other: 4%

Christian: 34%

Top Landmarks

The Basilica of Our Lady of Peace

Sudanese-style mosques

Taï National Park

Glossary

cassava—a root vegetable shaped like a tube

ethnic—related to races or large groups of people who share things such as customs, religion, and language

festival—a time or event of celebration

grasslands—lands covered with grasses and other soft plants with few bushes or trees

humid—having a lot of water in the air

independence—freedom from being under control of someone or something

Indigenous—related to people originally from an area

plantain—a banana-like fruit that is commonly cooked

rainforests—thick forests that get a lot of rain

To Learn More

AT THE LIBRARY

Kenney, Karen Latchana. *Rain Forests*. Minneapolis, Minn.: Bellwether Media, 2022.

Lesley, John. *Africa*. Sydney, Aus.: Redback Publishing, 2025.

Orr, Tamra. *Awesome Animals of Africa*. Mount Joy, Pa.: Curious Fox Books, 2024.

ON THE WEB

FACTSURFER

Factsurfer.com gives you a safe, fun way to find more information.

1. Go to www.factsurfer.com.
2. Enter "Ivory Coast" into the search box and click 🔍.
3. Select your book cover to see a list of related content.

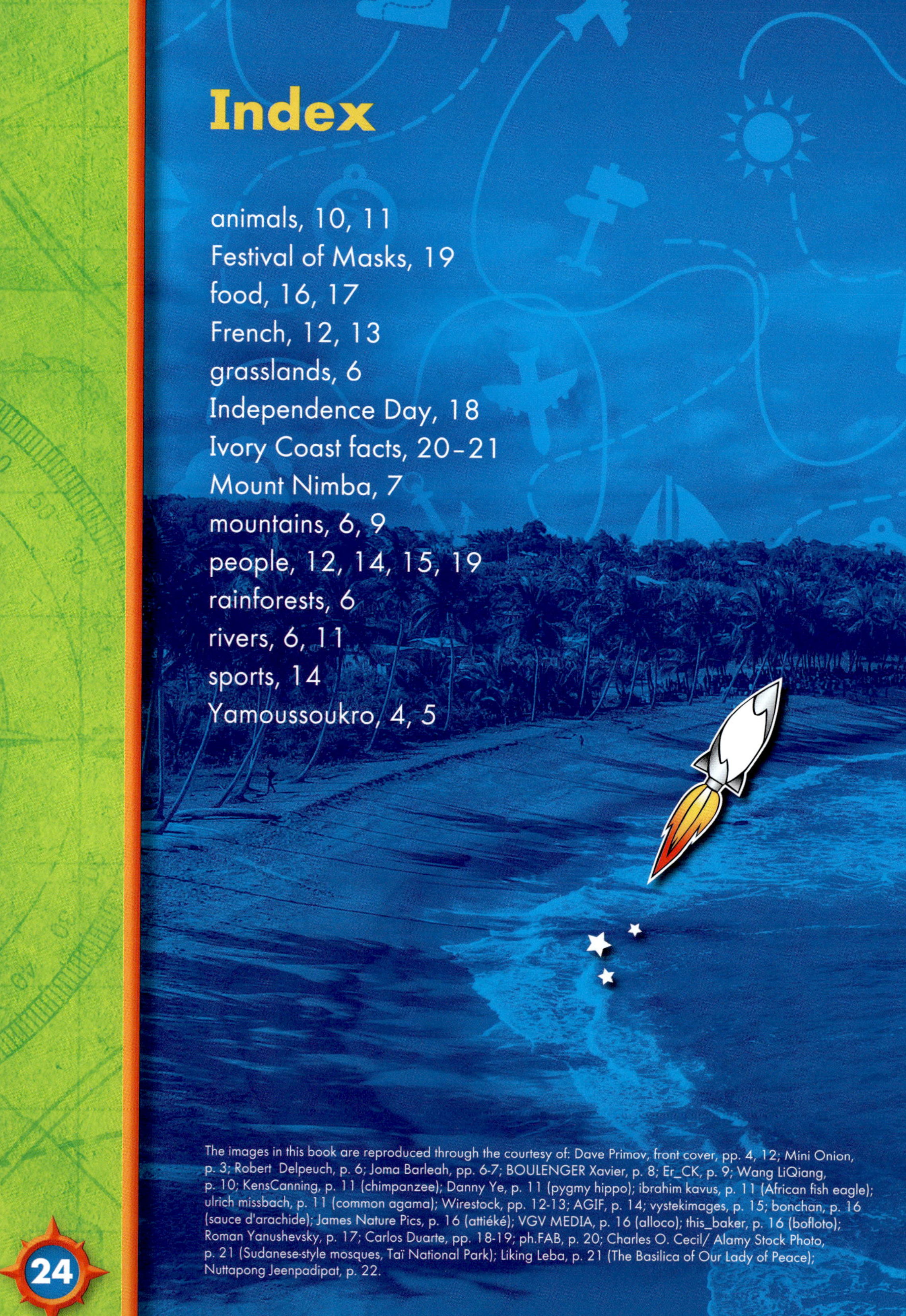

Index

The images in this book are reproduced through the courtesy of: Dave Primov, front cover, pp. 4, 12; Mini Onion, p. 3; Robert Delpeuch, p. 6; Joma Barleah, pp. 6-7; BOULENGER Xavier, p. 8; Er_CK, p. 9; Wang LiQiang, p. 10; KensCanning, p. 11 (chimpanzee); Danny Ye, p. 11 (pygmy hippo); ibrahim kavus, p. 11 (African fish eagle); ulrich missbach, p. 11 (common agama); Wirestock, pp. 12-13; AGIF, p. 14; vystekimages, p. 15; bonchan, p. 16 (sauce d'arachide); James Nature Pics, p. 16 (attiéké); VGV MEDIA, p. 16 (alloco); this_baker, p. 16 (bofloto); Roman Yanushevsky, p. 17; Carlos Duarte, pp. 18-19; ph.FAB, p. 20; Charles O. Cecil/ Alamy Stock Photo, p. 21 (Sudanese-style mosques, Taï National Park); Liking Leba, p. 21 (The Basilica of Our Lady of Peace); Nuttapong Jeenpadipat, p. 22.